cocktails &
appetizers

WILLIAMS-SONOMA

cocktails & appetizers

WELDON OWEN

contents

1

2

introduction

The cocktail is a quintessentially American invention, a remarkable coming together of disparate ingredients to create singular drinks. And the cocktail party is perhaps the most American form of entertaining. Whether held during the transitional hours between work and dinner or as a leisurely weekend gathering, a cocktail party offers a chance for easy social interaction. It can be as elegant and lavish or as casual, even spare, as you like. Dishes inspired by different cuisines mix easily in a cocktail spread. Guests can nibble daintily or make a meal of appetizers as they mingle.

—chuck williams

cold drinks

The seductive sound of ice chattering in a silver cocktail shaker heralds the arrival of

a refreshingly chilled libation. More than a mere mixed drink, at its best the cocktail

is an art form—ingenious, adaptable, and delicious. When spirits combine with one

another or with exotic juices, the sum of the parts is shaken or stirred to new heights

of refreshment. Whether at the end of a hard day or at the heart of an endless

summer, a cocktail can stimulate the palate, lift the spirits, and reinvigorate the mind.

Rum Rumba

With the rims of the serving glasses rubbed with lemon and crusted in sugar, this drink satisfies a sweet tooth. For a splash of brilliant color, swirl in a few drops of pomegranate molasses, available in Middle Eastern grocery stores.

sugar for coating rims of glasses

1 lemon slice

¾ cup (6 fl oz/180 ml) golden rum

¾ cup (6 fl oz/180 ml) pineapple juice

¾ cup (6 fl oz/180 ml) orange juice

juice of 2 limes

Angostura bitters

SERVES 3

1 Sprinkle sugar on a plate. Rub lemon slice on rims of cocktail glasses and dip each glass in sugar.

2 In a shaker, combine rum, pineapple juice, orange juice, and lime juice with 6 or 7 ice cubes. Shake well and strain into prepared glasses. Top each drink with a splash of Angostura bitters.

Sangria

½ *each* lemon and orange, sliced and seeded

½ apple, cored and sliced

½ cup (2 oz/60 g) fresh strawberries, hulled and sliced

¼ cup (2 oz/60 g) sugar

1 bottle (24 fl oz/750 ml) dry red wine

3 tablespoons (1½ fl oz/45 ml) brandy

soda water

SERVES 6

Sangria is the beloved Spanish infusion of red wine and fruit. This recipe adds strawberries to the mix. When choosing the wine, look for something dry and of good quality. Choose one you would drink by itself.

1 Place lemon, orange, apple, strawberries, and sugar in a large pitcher.

2 Pour in wine and brandy and stir with a long-handled spoon. Refrigerate for 1 hour.

3 Just before serving, add up to 2 cups (16 fl oz/500 ml) soda water. Stir again and serve over ice in tall glasses.

White-Wine Sangria

¼ cup (2 oz/60 g) sugar

2 cinnamon sticks

handful fresh mint leaves

1 *each* lemon and blood orange

1 peach, pitted, peeled, and sliced

½ bottle (12 fl oz/375 ml) dry white wine

soda water

SERVES 6

This may be the best wine cooler you've ever had. Afloat not only with fresh fruit such as citrus and peaches, it is also infused with cinnamon sticks and fresh mint. Although blood oranges add a beautiful color to the white wine, regular oranges work just as well.

1 In a saucepan, combine ⅔ cup (5 fl oz/ 160 ml) water, sugar, cinnamon sticks, and half of the mint. Bring to a boil over medium heat and simmer for 5 minutes. Let cool.

2 Slice the lemon and orange. Place lemon, orange, and peach slices in a pitcher. Add wine, sugar mixture, and remaining mint. Fill pitcher with soda water. Stir well. Pour over ice cubes in tall glasses, adding some fruit to each glass.

Rum Pineapple Punch

Watch out for this deceptively easy-to-drink cocktail. Its ratio of pineapple to rum is two to one. Be sure to use fresh pineapple, not canned. Its flavor makes all the difference.

SUGAR SYRUP

½ cup (4 oz/125 g) sugar

1 cup (8 fl oz/250 ml) golden rum

3 fresh pineapple slices, chopped

2¼ cups (18 fl oz/560 ml) pineapple juice

SERVES 4

1 FOR SUGAR SYRUP: In a small saucepan, combine sugar and ½ cup (4 fl oz/125 ml) water and stir until sugar is dissolved. Bring to a rolling boil over high heat. Reduce heat to a simmer and cook until a light syrup is formed, about 5 minutes. Remove from heat and let cool.

2 In a pitcher, combine rum, chopped pineapple, and 2 splashes of sugar syrup. Let stand for 30 minutes. Add pineapple juice and stir well. To serve, pour over crushed ice in tall glasses.

Blue Hawaiian

This popular drink is made with blue curaçao, an orange-flavored liqueur made from the dried peel of bitter oranges found on the Caribbean island of Curaçao. The result is a rather unworldly, creamy blue concoction.

¼ cup (2 fl oz/60 ml) light rum

¼ cup (2 fl oz/60 ml) blue curaçao

¼ cup (2 fl oz/60 ml) coconut cream (see note, top of page 39)

½ cup (4 fl oz/125 ml) pineapple juice

SERVES 3

1 In a blender, combine rum, curaçao, coconut cream, and pineapple juice with 1½ cups (12 fl oz/375 ml) crushed ice. Blend on high speed until combined. Pour into martini glasses.

Negroni

3 tablespoons (1½ fl oz/45 ml) gin

3 tablespoons (1½ fl oz/45 ml)
sweet vermouth

3 tablespoons (1½ fl oz/45 ml)
Campari

1 orange slice or twist

SERVES 1

Americans are masters of the cocktail, but Italians have some classics, too. Take the Negroni—the potent drink that mixes gin and sweet vermouth with Campari (see note, top of page 31), a combination that's credited to a 1920s cocktail-loving Florentine aristocrat. At Harry's Bar in Venice, they make a perfect Negroni—this is their recipe.

1 Pour gin, vermouth, and Campari into a glass half-filled with ice cubes. Stir briefly to mix. Add orange slice or twist. Alternatively, in an ice-filled shaker, combine gin, vermouth, and Campari. Shake and strain into a chilled glass. Add orange slice or twist.

Bellini

SUGAR SYRUP

½ cup (4 oz/125 g) sugar

2 ripe white peaches, peeled, pitted, and chopped

1 bottle (24 fl oz/750 ml) dry Prosecco, well chilled

SERVES 8

One of the world's great aperitifs, the Bellini—a simple but sublime concoction of white peach purée and Prosecco, an Italian sparkling wine—was created at Harry's Bar in Venice. The sugar syrup in this recipe is optional, depending on the sweetness of the peaches.

1 FOR SUGAR SYRUP: In a small saucepan, combine sugar and ½ cup (4 fl oz/125 ml) water and stir until sugar is dissolved. Bring to a rolling boil over high heat. Reduce heat to a simmer and cook until a light syrup is formed, about 5 minutes. Remove from heat and let cool.

2 Pass chopped peaches through a food mill placed over a bowl. Pass coarse peach purée through a fine-mesh sieve placed over a bowl, pressing on the solids with the back of a spoon. Taste and adjust sweetness, if needed, with a little sugar syrup. Cover purée and refrigerate until well chilled.

3 In a pitcher, combine peach purée and Prosecco. Stir until well blended. Pour into well-chilled glasses.

The Perfect Mint Julep

40 small fresh spearmint leaves,
plus 12–15 sprigs for garnish

6 tablespoons (3 fl oz/90 ml)
bourbon whiskey, preferably
Maker's Mark, plus 3 cups
(24 fl oz/750 ml)

1 cup (8 fl oz/250 ml)
distilled water

1 cup (8 oz/250 g)
granulated sugar

confectioners' (icing) sugar
for dusting

SERVES 12–15

This Southern cocktail is required drinking at the Kentucky Derby and any parties associated with it. A debate rages: Should the mint be bruised or not? In this rendition, the drink is infused with bruised mint leaves and then served with whole sprigs.

1 Put mint leaves in a small bowl with 6 tablespoons bourbon. Let soak for 15 minutes. Gather up mint in a square of cheesecloth (muslin) and wring bundle over bowl. Dip bundle in liquid and wring again. Repeat dipping and wringing process several times. Discard bundle. Set mint extract aside.

2 In a small saucepan, bring distilled water to a simmer over medium-high heat. Add granulated sugar and stir constantly until sugar is completely dissolved. Remove from heat and let syrup cool to room temperature.

3 In a pitcher, combine 3 cups bourbon and 1 cup (8 fl oz/250 ml) syrup. Add mint extract to pitcher 1 tablespoon at a time, tasting as you go, until mixture has a soft mint aroma and flavor, using about 3 tablespoons total of mint extract. Cover julep mixture tightly with a lid or plastic wrap and refrigerate until flavors marry, about 24 hours.

4 To serve, fill glasses halfway with shaved ice. Insert a mint sprig in each glass and then pack in more shaved ice to about 1 inch (2.5 cm) above rim. Insert a straw cut to reach 1 inch (2.5 cm) above rim. When frost forms on surface of glasses, pour julep mixture over ice and add a dusting of confectioners' sugar.

Campari Grapefruit Frappé

Campari is a popular Italian brand of bitters, a blend of alcohol, spices, and herbs. Here, it's mixed with ruby red grapefruit juice, along with an invigorating punch of homemade fresh ginger syrup.

¼ cup (2 oz/60 g) sugar

1-inch (2.5-cm) piece fresh ginger, peeled and thinly sliced

½ cup (4 fl oz/125 ml) Campari

2 cups (16 fl oz/500 ml) ruby red grapefruit juice

1 lime, thinly sliced

SERVES 4

1 In a small saucepan, bring ¼ cup (2 fl oz/60 ml) water to a simmer over low heat. Add sugar and ginger and stir until sugar is dissolved. Remove from heat and let steep until syrup is room temperature. Discard ginger.

2 In a shaker, combine Campari, grapefruit juice, and lime slices. Add ginger syrup to taste and crushed ice. Shake and pour immediately into individual glasses.

Pisco Sour

A grape brandy from South America, Pisco is distilled from Muscat grapes and usually is aged for only a few months in clay containers. Although this is not a smooth spirit, it does bear more fruit flavors than other briefly aged brandies. Its name comes from the Peruvian seaport town of Pisco, located near the region where the grapes are grown.

SUGAR SYRUP

½ cup (4 oz/125 g) sugar

½ cup (4 fl oz/125 ml) Pisco brandy

3 tablespoons (1½ fl oz/45 ml) fresh lemon juice

2 egg whites

4 dashes of Angostura bitters

SERVES 2

1 FOR SUGAR SYRUP: In a small saucepan, combine sugar and ½ cup (4 fl oz/125 ml) water and stir until sugar is dissolved. Bring to a rolling boil over high heat. Reduce heat to a simmer and cook until a light syrup is formed, about 5 minutes. Remove from heat and let cool.

2 Fill a shaker two-thirds full with ice cubes. Pour in Pisco brandy, lemon juice, 2 tablespoons sugar syrup, egg whites, and bitters. Shake well. Strain into chilled cocktail glasses or serve over ice.

Rum-Cranberry Fizz

Try serving this sophisticated combination in a chilled martini glass—it provides a nice change from the ever-popular cranberry juice-based cosmopolitan. Look for ruby red grapefruit juice, or whole fruits if you're squeezing your own, for the brightest color and sweetest taste.

¼ cup (2 fl oz/60 ml) white rum

¼ cup (2 fl oz/60 ml) cranberry juice

¼ cup (2 fl oz/60 ml) grapefruit juice

soda water

SERVES 1

1 In a shaker, combine rum, cranberry juice, and grapefruit juice with 4 or 5 ice cubes. Shake well and strain into a cocktail glass. Top with a splash of soda water.

Mai Tai

This mai tai recipe is less sweet than many bar versions. If you prefer a sweeter cocktail, add more orgeat syrup to taste. If you can't find orgeat syrup, you can make it by flavoring simple syrup with one or two drops of pure almond extract.

¼ cup (2 fl oz/60 ml) dark rum

¼ cup (2 fl oz/60 ml) golden rum

¼ cup (2 fl oz/60 ml) fresh lime juice, plus ½ lime

splash of apricot brandy

dash of orgeat syrup

SERVES 1

1 In a shaker, combine dark rum, golden rum, ¼ cup lime juice, apricot brandy, orgeat syrup, and 3 or 4 ice cubes. Shake well and strain into a cocktail glass. Squeeze juice of ½ lime on top.

Guava Colada

This mild, thick, pale pink cocktail is an ultra-tropical twist on the piña colada. Coconut cream is a canned, sweetened product not to be confused with canned coconut milk; it can be purchased in many grocery stores.

½ cup (4 fl oz/125 ml) golden rum

½ cup (4 fl oz/125 ml) guava juice

¼ cup (2 fl oz/60 ml) coconut cream

2 tablespoons heavy (double) cream

2 fresh guava slices

SERVES 2

1 In a blender, combine rum, guava juice, coconut cream, and heavy cream with 2 cups (16 fl oz/500 ml) crushed ice. Blend until thick and frothy.

2 Pour into cocktail glasses. Garnish each glass with a guava slice.

Goal Post

The Grafton Street Pub in Boston serves up this signature drink, proving that a heady pint of Guinness isn't the only choice in an Irish pub.

2 tablespoons (1 fl oz/30 ml) Triple Sec

¼ cup (2 fl oz/60 ml) Absolut Citron

1 tablespoon (½ fl oz/15 ml) Essencia Orange Muscat

1 tablespoon (½ fl oz/15 ml) Chambord

sour mix

SERVES 1

1 In a shaker, combine Triple Sec, Absolut Citron, orange muscat, and Chambord. Shake and pour over ice in a cocktail glass. Top with sour mix to taste.

Moscow Mule

Dating to the 1940s, this is said to be one of the first vodka-based drinks to catch on in the United States. Look for nonalcoholic ginger beer – its flavor is much stronger than ginger ale.

3 tablespoons (1½ fl oz/45 ml) vodka

juice of ½ lime

¾–1 cup (6–8 fl oz/180–250 ml) ginger beer or ginger ale

1 lime slice

SERVES 1

1 Place ice cubes in a highball glass. Pour vodka and lime juice over ice. Fill with ginger beer, stir, and add lime slice.

Dune Cocktail

This pale turquoise drink matches the color of the water outside the Ocean Club on Paradise Island in the Bahamas. It's made with cream of coconut, a sweet mixture that is not the same as coconut cream (see note, top of page 39). Cream of coconut can be found in many supermarkets, or you can make it yourself, following this recipe.

CREAM OF COCONUT

1 can (14 fl oz/430 ml) unsweetened coconut milk

⅓ cup (3 oz/90 g) sugar

2 tablespoons (1 fl oz/30 ml) gin

1 tablespoon (½ fl oz/15 ml) Cointreau

splash of blue curaçao

SERVES 1

1 FOR CREAM OF COCONUT: In a saucepan over low heat, simmer unsweetened coconut milk with sugar, stirring, until sugar is dissolved. Remove from heat and let cool.

2 In an ice-filled shaker, combine gin, Cointreau, curaçao, and 6 tablespoons (3 fl oz/90 ml) cream of coconut. Strain into a cocktail glass.

Bahama Mama

There are as many variations of this creamy red tropical elixir as there are bartenders. This recipe is made without coffee liqueur.

6 tablespoons (3 fl oz/90 ml) dark rum

2 tablespoons (1 fl oz/30 ml) Triple Sec

¼ cup (2 fl oz/60 ml) orange juice

¼ cup (2 fl oz/60 ml) pineapple juice

splash of grenadine

splash of cream of coconut (above)

SERVES 2

1 In an ice-filled shaker, combine dark rum, Triple Sec, orange and pineapple juices, grenadine, and cream of coconut. Strain into hurricane glasses.

Vodka Lemonade

Making lemonade from scratch adds quite a bit of zest to this simple, refreshing cocktail. Store-bought all-natural lemonade can be substituted in a pinch.

SUGAR SYRUP

½ cup (4 oz/125 g) sugar

LEMONADE

¼ cup (2 fl oz/60 ml) fresh lemon juice

¾–1 cup (6–8 fl oz/180–250 ml) cold water

½ cup (4 fl oz/125 ml) vodka

1 lemon, cut into ¼-inch (6-mm) slices

2 fresh mint sprigs for garnish

SERVES 2

1 FOR SUGAR SYRUP: In a small saucepan, combine sugar and ½ cup (4 fl oz/125 ml) water and stir until sugar is dissolved. Bring to a rolling boil over high heat. Reduce heat to a simmer and cook until a light syrup is formed, about 5 minutes. Remove from heat and let cool.

2 FOR LEMONADE: In a large glass measuring cup or pitcher, combine lemon juice, cold water, and 1 tablespoon sugar syrup. Stir well.

3 Pour vodka and lemonade into a shaker and shake well. Fill 2 tall glasses with ice cubes and divide lemon slices between them. Pour vodka-lemonade mixture into glasses. Garnish with mint sprigs.

hot drinks

A hot drink is the perfect antidote to chilly winter weather. Spiced and sweetened, these fruity, welcoming beverages warm the heart and the hands. Hot drinks were popular in America's Colonial times, but the roots of these restorative liquids lie in Northern European nations—from Britain, or more particularly Scotland, comes the toddy, while Scandinavia has given us glögg. These time-honored concoctions offer heat, comfort, and companionship. So gather round the fire with friends and nurse a beaker on a long winter's night.

Hot Buttered Rum

Dark rum's rich and spicy flavor suits this time-honored recipe. Some versions call for the butter to float on top, but it's best stirred right into the warm rum. Like all good hot drinks, this is easily made in large quantities for a crowd.

1 teaspoon sugar

3 whole cloves

¼ cup (2 fl oz/60 ml) dark rum

whole nutmeg for grating

1 teaspoon unsalted butter

½ cinnamon stick

SERVES 1

1 Combine sugar, cloves, and rum in a tumbler or mug. Add ½ cup (4 fl oz/ 125 ml) boiling water.

2 Grate nutmeg to taste over top. Add butter and stir briefly with cinnamon stick. Serve immediately.

RESERVE
Calvados
DOMAINE FAMILIAL L. DUPONT
www.calvados-dupont.com

Hot Toddy

This British classic was originally served cold, until sailors decided to heat it up to keep warm. It's the perfect restorative drink following an afternoon of wintertime activities.

¼ cup (2 fl oz/60 ml) Scotch whisky

3 or 4 whole cloves

zest of 1 lemon, cut in a long spiral strip

1 teaspoon honey

2 tablespoons fresh lemon juice

SERVES 1

1 In a glass, combine whisky, cloves, and lemon zest.

2 Add honey, lemon juice, and ½ cup (4 fl oz/125 ml) boiling water. Stir well. Serve immediately.

Apple Toddy

The French take on the hot toddy uses Calvados or applejack brandy, along with apple syrup, giving the drink a sweeter scent and flavor than the English original. When buying apple syrup, look for the Austrian brand D'Arbo; this company produces some of the best, most intense fruit syrups on the market.

¼ cup (2 fl oz/60 ml) Calvados or applejack brandy

¼ cup (2 fl oz/60 ml) apple syrup

4 or 5 thin apple slices

whole nutmeg for grating

SERVES 1

1 In a glass, combine Calvados and apple syrup. Add ¼–½ cup (2–4 fl oz/ 60–125 ml) boiling water and stir.

2 Add apple slices and grate nutmeg to taste over top. Serve immediately.

Glögg

½ cup (4 oz/125 g) sugar

1 bottle (12 fl oz/375 ml) brandy

8 whole cloves

½ cup (3 oz/90 g) raisins

½ cup (2½ oz/75 g) slivered blanched almonds

1 cup (8 fl oz/250 ml) ruby Port

SERVES 6

This Scandinavian party punch is served hot and sweetened with sugar or simple syrup. The syrup will keep indefinitely in the refrigerator and is useful for sweetening many kinds of punch as well as iced tea and cocktails.

1 In a large, nonaluminum saucepan with a lid, bring ½ cup (4 fl oz/125 ml) water to a simmer, uncovered, over medium-high heat. Add sugar and stir constantly until it completely dissolves.

2 Reduce heat to low, add brandy, cloves, raisins, and almonds, and stir to combine. Cook, uncovered, over low heat until warm, but not boiling.

3 Averting your face, carefully ignite brandy mixture with a match. Allow it to flame for about 20 seconds. Add Port and stir with a wooden spoon until flames subside. If flames do not subside, cover saucepan with lid to extinguish.

4 Pour mixture into a serving pitcher and then ladle into small glasses.

vegetables, eggs & cheese

Fritters, croquettes, and tartlets are among the fresh and imaginative vegetarian offerings that pair so well with drinks. In these recipes, cheese and vegetables are culinary chameleons, disguised in coatings of crispy bread crumbs or buttery pastry or hidden within balls of risotto. The classics are revisited, given a lively twist with additions of fresh herbs. Whether the flavors and forms are familiar or new, each bite provides a panoply of tastes and textures, just what is needed to accompany drinks.

Zucchini and Spinach Tartlets

CRUNCH DOUGH

1¼ cups (6½ oz/200 g) all-purpose (plain) flour

¼ teaspoon sugar

¾ teaspoon salt

6 tablespoons (3 oz/90 g) cold unsalted butter, cut into ½-inch (12-mm) cubes

FILLING

2 tablespoons olive oil

¾ lb (375 g) spinach, large stems removed

salt

4 tablespoons (2 oz/60 g) unsalted butter

2 zucchini (courgettes), trimmed and cut into slices ⅛ inch (3 mm) thick

freshly ground black pepper

½ cup (2½ oz/75 g) pine nuts

6 tablespoons (3 fl oz/90 ml) crème fraîche

1 egg yolk

2 tablespoons milk

MAKES 6 TARTLETS

The buttery crunch dough produces a short crust, which is ideal for these tartlets. The dough is best made a day ahead and refrigerated overnight.

1 FOR DOUGH: In bowl of a stand mixer fitted with paddle attachment, combine flour, sugar, and salt on low speed. Add half of butter and combine until pea-sized pieces form, about 30 seconds. Add remaining butter and combine as before. Stir in ⅓ cup (3 fl oz/80 ml) cold water and mix until large lumps form.

2 Transfer mixture to a lightly floured work surface. Using your hands, bring mixture together to form a rough dough. Gently knead with heel of your hand, about 20 seconds. Flatten to a disk, wrap in plastic wrap, and refrigerate for at least 1 hour or preferably overnight.

3 Divide crunch dough into 6 equal pieces. On a lightly floured work surface, roll out each piece into a round about 7 inches (18 cm) in diameter. Place dough rounds between pieces of waxed paper and refrigerate for at least 1 hour.

4 FOR FILLING: In a large saucepan, heat olive oil over medium-high heat. Add spinach, season with salt, and cook, stirring, until leaves are wilted and dark green, 3–5 minutes. Drain and let cool. Gently squeeze out any excess moisture and coarsely chop.

5 In a large skillet, melt 2 tablespoons butter over medium-high heat. Add zucchini, season with salt and pepper, and cook, stirring, until just softened and liquid is released, about 3 minutes. Transfer to paper towels to drain.

6 Preheat oven to 350°F (180°C). In a baking dish, spread pine nuts in a single layer. Toast, stirring often, until nuts are golden, 5–7 minutes. Spread on a plate and let cool. Raise oven temperature to 425°F (220°C). Line a baking sheet with parchment (baking) paper.

7 In a bowl, combine spinach, zucchini, and pine nuts. Adjust seasonings. Divide filling among rolled-out pastries, placing a mound in center of each. Top each with 1 tablespoon crème fraîche. Cut remaining 2 tablespoons butter into small pieces and divide evenly among tarts. Fold pastry up around filling to form sides, and pinch corners. Transfer to prepared baking sheet. Cover with plastic wrap and refrigerate for 1 hour.

8 In a small bowl, beat egg yolk with milk. Brush pastry sides with egg wash. Bake until crust is golden, 20–30 minutes. Serve hot or at room temperature.

Supplì al Telefono

3 cups (24 fl oz/750 ml) vegetable stock or chicken stock

½ cup (2½ oz/75 g) drained, oil-packed, sun-dried tomatoes

2 tablespoons olive oil

1 clove garlic, crushed

1 cup (7 oz/220 g) Carnaroli rice

¼ cup (2 fl oz/60 ml) dry white wine

salt and freshly ground black pepper

½ cup (4 fl oz/125 ml) heavy (double) cream

2 tablespoons unsalted butter

½ cup (2 oz/60 g) grated Parmesan cheese

¾ cup (1 oz/30 g) basil leaves, torn into small pieces

¼ lb (125 g) fresh mozzarella, drained and cut into ¼-inch (6-mm) dice

½ cup (2½ oz/75 g) all-purpose (plain) flour

2 eggs, beaten

1½–2 cups (6–8 oz/185–250 g) fine dried white bread crumbs

vegetable oil for deep-frying

MAKES 24 RICE BALLS

Risotto balls can be made with Carnaroli, Arborio, or any other member of the starchy, short-grain rice family. This enchanting dish is named for the telephone line–like strands of cheese that form when the balls are bitten into.

1 In a saucepan, bring stock to a gentle simmer. Meanwhile, cut the sun-dried tomatoes into strips and set aside.

2 In a heavy-bottomed risotto pan or sauté pan, heat olive oil over medium-low heat and gently sauté garlic until just soft. Stir in rice and cook for 2 minutes until rice is coated with oil, is partially transparent, and begins to make a clicking noise. Quickly add wine and stir constantly until liquid is absorbed.

3 Add stock a ladleful at a time, stirring constantly until liquid is absorbed before next addition. When half of stock has been added, stir in sun-dried tomatoes and season to taste with salt and pepper. Continue adding stock in same manner, followed by cream, until rice is al dente.

4 Remove from heat and stir in butter, Parmesan, and basil. Cover pan and let stand for 3 minutes. Uncover pan and stir. Taste and adjust seasoning if needed. Spread risotto in a shallow dish and let cool completely.

5 Shape 1 tablespoon cooled risotto into a walnut-sized ball molded around 1 mozzarella cube. Repeat to make 24 balls.

6 Spread flour on a plate. Beat eggs in a shallow bowl. Spread bread crumbs on another plate. Coat rice balls first in flour, then eggs, and finally bread crumbs.

7 In a deep skillet, pour vegetable oil to a depth of 3 inches (7.5 cm) and heat to 350°F (180°C) on a deep-frying thermometer. Cook rice balls in batches of 4 until golden all over, 2–3 minutes. If cooked too quickly, cheese in middle will not melt. Drain on paper towels and keep warm in a low oven while cooking remaining rice balls. Serve warm.

Egg Salad with Chervil and Chives

If chervil is not available, substitute 2 teaspoons chopped fresh tarragon. Serve atop slices of brown country bread, garnished with more chives. For a different flavor, top with fresh watercress sprigs.

6 eggs, at room temperature

3 tablespoons finely chopped fresh chives

2 tablespoons finely chopped fresh chervil

⅓ cup (3 fl oz/80 ml) mayonnaise, or to taste

1½ teaspoons Dijon mustard

salt and freshly ground black pepper

vinegar or lemon juice

SERVES 4–6

1 Put eggs in a saucepan of cold water to cover. Bring to a boil and cook for 1 minute. Turn off heat, cover, and let stand for 6 minutes. Remove eggs and immerse in cold water until cool.

2 Peel eggs and mash coarsely in a bowl. Add chives, chervil, mayonnaise, and mustard and season with salt and pepper. Add a few drops of vinegar or lemon juice to taste.

Wild Mushroom and Goat Cheese Tartlets

Look for log-shaped goat cheese that has been aged. It has a dry, edible rind, slices easily, and softens as it bakes.

1 recipe Crunch Dough (page 59)

18 oz (560 g) mushrooms such as cremini and chanterelle

1 tablespoon unsalted butter

2 tablespoons olive oil

salt and freshly ground black pepper

¾ cup (6 fl oz/180 ml) crème fraîche

½ lb (250 g) aged goat cheese log, cut into 16 slices

4 tablespoons (⅓ oz/10 g) snipped fresh chives

MAKES 8 TARTLETS

1 Place 8 tartlet rings, each 3 inches (7.5 cm) in diameter and about ¾ inch (2 cm) deep, on a baking sheet lined with parchment (baking) paper. Divide crunch dough into 8 equal pieces. On a lightly floured work surface, roll out each piece ¼ inch (6 mm) thick and use to line a tartlet ring. Trim edges. Using a fork, prick bases. Cover with plastic wrap and refrigerate for at least 1 hour.

2 Preheat oven to 425°F (220°C). To blind bake pastry, line chilled pastry shells with aluminum foil, parchment (baking) paper, or waxed paper. Fill with pie weights or uncooked beans or rice. Bake for 10 minutes, then remove lining and weights. Return shells to oven and bake until bottoms are dry and edges are golden, about 5 minutes longer.

3 FOR FILLING: Select 8 small, attractive mushrooms to garnish top of tarts. Wipe them clean and set aside. Slice remaining mushrooms. In a saucepan, melt butter in olive oil over medium-high heat. Add sliced mushrooms and cook, stirring often, until mushrooms have released their liquid and most of it has evaporated, about 10 minutes. Season with salt and pepper. Remove from heat and let cool.

4 Spread 1 tablespoon crème fraîche in each tart shell and top with cooked mushrooms and 2 slices goat cheese. Garnish each with a reserved whole mushroom. Season with salt and pepper and sprinkle each with 1½ teaspoons chives. Divide remaining ¼ cup (2 fl oz/60 ml) crème fraîche evenly among tarts, dotting the tops. Bake until crust is golden and filling is bubbling, 25–30 minutes. Serve warm.

Crispy Breaded Tomato Slices

Crisp on the outside but warm and juicy inside, these tomato appetizers can also be served as a delicious side dish or as a simple lunch with salad.

4 or 5 slices white or whole-wheat (wholemeal) bread, crusts removed

salt and freshly ground black pepper

1 cup (5 oz/155 g) all-purpose (plain) flour

1 egg

1 teaspoon milk or heavy (double) cream

3 tomatoes, cored and cut into 12 slices total, each about ½ inch (12 mm) thick

2–3 tablespoons unsalted butter or olive oil, plus more if needed

¼ lb (125 g) fresh mozzarella cheese, cut into 12 slices about ⅛ inch (3 mm) thick

1 scant tablespoon chopped fresh marjoram

SERVES 2–4

1 In a food processor, process bread into fine crumbs. You should have about 1½ cups (3 oz/90 g). Season with salt and pepper.

2 Spread flour on a large plate. Beat egg with milk in a shallow bowl. Spread seasoned bread crumbs on another plate. Dip tomato slices first in flour, then egg mixture, and finally bread crumbs.

3 In a large nonstick skillet over medium heat, melt 2–3 tablespoons butter or heat 2–3 tablespoons olive oil. When hot, add tomatoes and cook, covered, until browned on undersides, 3–5 minutes. Uncover pan and turn over tomatoes, adding more butter or oil if needed, to brown other side. Lay 1 mozzarella slice over each tomato and re-cover pan. Cook until second side is browned and cheese is melted, 3–5 minutes. Remove from heat and transfer to a warmed platter. Garnish with chopped marjoram. Serve at once.

Deviled Eggs with Red Onion and Dill

To dress up these classic hors d'oeuvres, top the eggs with a smattering of smoked Spanish paprika and capers, or make them with tiny quail eggs.

¼ cup (1¼ oz/37 g) finely chopped red onion

2 tablespoons white wine vinegar

6 eggs, at room temperature

2–3 tablespoons mayonnaise

1 tablespoon Dijon mustard

1 tablespoon snipped fresh chives

pinch of cayenne pepper

2 tablespoons finely chopped fresh dill

salt and freshly ground black pepper

SERVES 6

1 In a small bowl, toss onion with 1 tablespoon vinegar. Set aside.

2 Put eggs in a saucepan of cold water to cover. Bring to a boil and cook for 1 minute. Turn off heat, cover, and let stand for 6 minutes. Remove eggs and immerse in cold water until cool.

3 Peel eggs and cut in half lengthwise. Scoop out yolks and mash them in a bowl with mayonnaise, mustard, chives, cayenne, remaining 1 tablespoon vinegar, half of onion mixture, and 1 tablespoon dill. Season to taste with salt and black pepper.

4 Spoon yolk mixture into egg whites. Garnish with remaining onion and dill.

Spicy Marinated Artichokes

These spicy baby artichokes are great to keep on hand for impromptu entertaining since they will last for a few weeks in the refrigerator. Serve them on toasted bread with goat cheese that has been marinated in a separate jar of this spicy oil.

FLAVORED OIL

2 cups (16 fl oz/500 ml) extra-virgin olive oil

4 fresh thyme sprigs

3 cloves garlic, unpeeled and smashed

3 strips lemon zest

½ teaspoon red pepper flakes

1 teaspoon whole black peppercorns

9 baby artichokes

juice of 1 lemon

salt and freshly ground black pepper

1 carrot, peeled and cut into sticks

1 yellow onion, cut into wedges

¼ cup (2 fl oz/60 ml) extra-virgin olive oil

1 cup (8 fl oz/250 ml) dry white wine

MAKES TWO ½-PINT
(8–FL OZ/250-ML) JARS

1 FOR FLAVORED OIL: In a small saucepan over low heat, combine olive oil, thyme, garlic, lemon zest, red pepper flakes, and black peppercorns. Gently warm until mixture is just heated; do not allow to bubble. Remove from heat and let cool uncovered.

2 Meanwhile, prepare artichokes. Fill a large bowl with cold water and lemon juice. Pull off outermost layer of tough leaves from artichokes. Peel and trim stems, removing ⅛ inch (3 mm) from each base. Cut each artichoke in half lengthwise and gently scoop out fuzzy choke. As each artichoke is prepared, submerge in lemon water to prevent discoloring. Drain artichokes and pat dry on paper towels. Season with salt and black pepper.

3 In a large sauté pan, arrange carrot and onion in a single layer and then arrange artichokes in another layer on top. Drizzle with olive oil and wine. Cook over high heat until mixture starts to bubble, then reduce heat to a simmer. Cover and cook until artichoke bases and leaves are tender, about 35 minutes. Remove from heat, let cool completely in pan, and then discard braising vegetables and pan juices.

4 Divide artichokes evenly between 2 sterilized ½-pint (8–fl oz/250-ml) jars. Pour in cooled flavored oil. Tightly seal jars and store in a cool, dark place for 3 days. Once jars are opened, store in refrigerator.

Spinach Empanadas with Aioli

PASTRY

2 cups (10 oz/315 g) all-purpose (plain) flour

9 tablespoons (4½ oz/140 g) cold unsalted butter, cut into small pieces

½ teaspoon salt

1 whole egg, plus 1 beaten egg yolk

FILLING

½ lb (250 g) spinach

2 tablespoons olive oil

1 red onion, finely chopped

1 tablespoon finely chopped garlic

2 tomatoes, peeled, seeded, and diced

¼ cup (1 oz/30 g) pine nuts

1 hard-boiled egg, peeled and chopped

½ teaspoon freshly grated nutmeg

salt and freshly ground black pepper

AIOLI

2–4 cloves garlic

⅛ teaspoon salt

2 teaspoons fresh lemon juice

1 egg yolk, at room temperature

¾ cup (6 fl oz/180 ml) olive oil

SERVES 4–6

You can prepare much of this dish before your guests arrive. Make the pastry dough days ahead and freeze it. Make the filling up to 1 day in advance and the aioli the day of serving. That leaves easy assembly and baking just before the doorbell rings.

1 FOR PASTRY: In a food processor, process flour, butter, and salt until it resembles coarse meal. With motor running, add whole egg. Pulse to blend, adding just enough water to bind into a crumbly dough. Transfer to a lightly floured work surface and form into a ball. Wrap in plastic wrap. Refrigerate for 30 minutes.

2 FOR FILLING: Stem and chop spinach. In a skillet, heat olive oil over medium-low heat. Add onion and garlic and cook, stirring often, until softened, 7–8 minutes. Add tomatoes and cook until softened, 5 minutes. Add spinach and pine nuts. Cook until spinach wilts, 5 minutes. Remove from heat. Stir in hard-boiled egg, nutmeg, and salt and pepper to taste. Let cool.

3 Preheat oven to 350°F (180°C). Line a rimmed baking sheet with parchment (baking) paper.

4 Divide dough in half. On a lightly floured work surface, roll out 1 portion of dough ⅛ inch (3 mm) thick. Using a 4-inch (10-cm) plain or fluted round cutter, cut out 9 rounds. Place 1 tablespoon filling on half of each round and brush edges with beaten egg yolk. Fold in half and pinch edges to seal. Repeat with remaining dough. Place empanadas on prepared baking sheet and brush with beaten egg yolk. Bake until golden, about 25 minutes.

5 FOR AIOLI: In a mortar, pound garlic, salt, and lemon juice to a paste with a pestle. Transfer to a food processor. Add egg yolk and process to blend. With machine running, add olive oil in a very thin stream to make an emulsified sauce. Serve for dipping alongside empanadas.

Vermont Butter and Cheese Chevrier

Orb Weaver Vermont Farmhouse Cheese

Shelburne Farms Cheddar

Vermont Shepherd

Stuffed Squash

½ lb (250 g) spinach, trimmed

2 tablespoons olive oil

½ cup (2½ oz/75 g) finely chopped yellow onion

2 eggs, beaten

2 tablespoons bread crumbs

½ cup (2 oz/60 g) shredded Mahón or Fontina cheese

¼ teaspoon salt

¼ teaspoon freshly ground black pepper

30 baby pattypan squashes

SERVES 4

This recipe makes more filling than you'll probably need. If you're having a large party, double the number of squashes. Otherwise, add a few more eggs and you have a great frittata mix.

1 Preheat oven to 400°F (200°C). Line a baking sheet with foil and grease lightly.

2 In a large pot of salted boiling water, blanch spinach for 5 seconds. Drain, rinse under cold water, squeeze well to dry, and chop finely. Set aside.

3 Heat olive oil in a skillet over medium-low heat. Add onion and sauté until lightly browned, about 10 minutes.

4 In a bowl, combine spinach, onion, eggs, bread crumbs, cheese, salt, and pepper. Set aside.

5 Slice off the stem end of each squash. Using a teaspoon, hollow out top half of each squash.

6 Stuff each squash with filling. Place squashes on prepared baking sheet. Bake until cooked through, about 20 minutes. Serve at once.

Crisp-Fried Baby Artichokes

Flattening the cleaned baby artichokes before frying, a classic technique, gives these appetizers an attractive, flowerlike presentation. Serve the olive paste (tapenade) in a bowl on the side or drizzled around the plate.

OLIVE PASTE

4 oz (125 g) Gaeta or Niçoise olives, pitted

2 cloves garlic

2 large anchovy fillets in oil, drained

1 tablespoon capers

pinch of dried thyme

pinch of cayenne pepper

2 tablespoons extra-virgin olive oil

1 tablespoon fresh lemon juice

12 baby artichokes

salt and freshly ground black pepper

vegetable oil for deep-frying

SERVES 4

1 FOR OLIVE PASTE: In a food processor, combine olives, garlic, anchovies, capers, thyme, and cayenne and process to coarsely chop. With machine running, pour olive oil in a steady stream into mixture. Finely chop but do not completely purée. Transfer to a bowl, taste and adjust seasoning if needed, and stir in lemon juice. Cover and set aside.

2 Trim stem of each artichoke, leaving about 1 inch (2.5 cm) intact. Gently ease each artichoke open. Scoop out fuzzy choke, if any, and discard. Invert artichokes and place on a cutting board. Flatten and spread out leaves by pushing down on base of each. Season with salt and black pepper.

3 In a deep pan, pour vegetable oil to a depth of 1½ inches (4 cm) and heat to 250°F (120°C) on a deep-frying thermometer. Add inverted artichokes to pan and gently cook, turning frequently, until base of each artichoke is tender when pierced with a sharp knife, 5–8 minutes. Carefully regulate heat to maintain oil temperature at 250°F (120°C) to prevent artichokes from frying too quickly. Transfer to paper towels to drain.

4 Transfer artichokes, still inverted, to cutting board and gently press on each base so leaves spread more. Raise oil temperature to 350°F (180°C). Return inverted artichokes to oil and cook for 1–2 minutes, then turn them right side up. Drain and serve hot or warm, with olive paste.

Guacamole

4 ripe avocados, pitted and peeled

1 sweet white onion such as Maui,
finely chopped

⅓ cup (½ oz/15 g) finely chopped
fresh cilantro (coriander)

1 serrano chile, seeded and chopped

juice of 2 limes

¼ cup (2 fl oz/60 ml) olive oil

salt and freshly ground
black pepper

SERVES 4

For a change of pace, serve guacamole with fried chips made of taro or yam. Rarely are avocados shipped ripe to supermarkets (they would bruise too easily), so if you're planning a big batch of guacamole, don't wait until the last minute. Make sure to give yourself a few days for the avocados to ripen. Putting them in a paper bag can expedite the process.

1 In a bowl, mash avocados with a fork. Stir in the remaining ingredients. Season to taste with salt and pepper. Mix well before serving.

Leek Fritters

Leeks, matzo, and walnuts make a tender and crisp fritter. These are easy to make and delicious served simply with a splash of lemon. The fritters are best cooked just before serving, but they can also be held in a warm oven.

3 lb (1.5 kg) leeks, including light green parts

4 matzos or 4 slices coarse country bread, crusts removed

3 eggs, lightly beaten

½ cup (2 oz/60 g) walnuts, chopped

1½ teaspoons salt, plus more to taste

½ teaspoon freshly ground black pepper

matzo meal

olive oil or vegetable oil for deep-frying

lemon wedges

MAKES ABOUT 16 FRITTERS

1 Cut leeks in half lengthwise, then cut crosswise into pieces ½ inch (12 mm) wide. Rinse well and drain. In a large saucepan, cook leeks in salted simmering water until very tender, about 20 minutes. Drain well. Squeeze out any excess liquid.

2 Soak matzos in water to cover until soft. Squeeze dry.

3 In a large bowl, combine leeks, matzos, eggs, walnuts, 1½ teaspoons salt, and pepper. Form into patties about 2 inches (5 cm) in diameter and ½–¾ inch (12 mm–2 cm) thick. If mixture seems too moist, add matzo meal until it holds together.

4 Spread matzo meal on a plate. Dip patties in it, coating both sides and tapping off excess.

5 In a large skillet, pour oil to a depth of 1 inch (2.5 cm) and heat to 350°F (180°C) on a deep-frying thermometer. When oil is hot, add patties in batches and fry, turning once, until golden brown, 3–4 minutes on each side. Using a slotted spatula, transfer to paper towels to drain. Sprinkle with salt and serve hot, with lemon wedges.

fish & shellfish

With their diverse yet sweet and succulent flavors, fish and shellfish are natural partners to many mixed drinks and are always popular as appetizers. They can be light or smoky, rich or briny. At their best they require only judicious seasoning, a touch of citrus or chile perhaps, to complement their freshness and enhance the taste of the sea. And the elegant presence of crab, scallops, smoked salmon, and, of course, caviar always brings a delightfully decadent touch of luxury to the party.

Andalusian Shrimp Fritters

These crisp pancakes are a specialty of Cádiz, where they are called *tortillitas de camarones*. They should be fried just before serving, and then garnished with lemon wedges.

1 yellow onion, finely chopped

6 tablespoons (⅓ oz/10 g) chopped fresh flat-leaf (Italian) parsley

2 tablespoons finely chopped fresh chives

⅔ lb (330 g) shrimp (prawns), peeled, deveined, and chopped

grated zest of 1 lemon

pinch of cayenne pepper

2 cups (10 oz/315 g) all-purpose (plain) flour

salt and freshly ground black pepper

olive oil for frying

lemon wedges

SERVES 6

1 In a bowl, combine onion, parsley, chives, shrimp, lemon zest, cayenne, and flour. Stir in 2½–3 cups (20–24 fl oz/ 625–750 ml) water to make a thick batter. Season with salt and black pepper. Cover and refrigerate for 3 hours.

2 In a large, heavy skillet, pour olive oil to a depth of ½ inch (12 mm) and heat over medium heat to 325°–350°F (165°–180°C) on a deep-frying thermometer. Drop in batter 1 tablespoon at a time and flatten with a metal spatula. Fry, turning once, until golden brown, 1½–2 minutes on each side. Drain briefly on paper towels. Sprinkle with salt and black pepper. Serve at once with lemon wedges.

Grilled Marinated Scallops with Lemon and Olive Oil

Simplicity itself, sea scallops are briefly marinated, then served with a Greek-style lemon and oil mixture. A grill's smoky flavor is part of the dish's appeal, but the skewers can also be broiled in a hot oven.

36 sea scallops, preferably day boat

¼ cup (2 fl oz/60 ml) olive oil

zest of 1 lemon, cut into broad strips

sea salt and freshly ground black pepper

DIPPING SAUCE

6 tablespoons (3 fl oz/90 ml) extra-virgin olive oil

juice of 1 lemon

sea salt and freshly ground black pepper

SERVES 6

1 Prepare a charcoal or gas grill for grilling over high heat. Soak 12 wooden skewers in water for about 30 minutes.

2 Remove tough side muscle from scallops, if present, then rinse and pat dry. In a glass bowl or dish, combine scallops with olive oil and lemon zest strips. Cover and marinate in refrigerator for 30 minutes.

3 FOR DIPPING SAUCE: In a bowl, combine extra-virgin olive oil and lemon juice. Season to taste with salt and pepper.

4 Thread 3 scallops onto each skewer. Season with salt and pepper. Grill until scallops are just barely cooked through, about 2 minutes on each side. Serve at once, with dipping sauce.

Oysters on the Half Shell

Buy your oysters from a reputable fishmonger on the same day that you plan to serve them. If possible, have the oysters shucked for you, making sure that you get the shells and the oyster liquid. If you shuck the oysters yourself, use only those that are firmly closed and scrub them well before opening.

CHAMPAGNE MIGNONETTE SAUCE

¾ cup (6 fl oz/180 ml) Champagne vinegar

6 tablespoons (2 oz/60 g) finely chopped shallots

¼ teaspoon kosher salt

¼ teaspoon freshly ground white pepper

MUSTARD DILL SAUCE

1 cup (250 g) mayonnaise

1 tablespoon Dijon mustard

3 tablespoons finely chopped fresh dill

2 teaspoons freshly grated lemon zest

freshly ground white pepper

36 raw oysters in the shell, well scrubbed

lemon wedges for serving

SERVES 6

1 FOR CHAMPAGNE MIGNONETTE SAUCE: In a small bowl, combine vinegar and shallots. Stir in salt and white pepper. Cover and refrigerate until ready to serve.

2 FOR MUSTARD DILL SAUCE: In a small bowl, combine mayonnaise, mustard, dill, and lemon zest. Season to taste with white pepper. Cover and refrigerate until ready to serve.

3 To shuck oysters, using an oyster glove or a kitchen towel, firmly hold an oyster steady on another towel on countertop. Gently ease point of oyster knife into hinge of shell (generally its narrowest part, where top and bottom shells join). Twist knife firmly to loosen top shell. Carefully slide knife around edge of shell to loosen it, without damaging oyster inside. Then pass knife along underside of top shell to loosen oyster. Remove top shell and pass knife under oyster to loosen it from bottom shell. Be careful not to spill liquid inside. Use a finger or cloth napkin to wipe around edge of bottom shell to clean away sand or broken pieces of shell.

4 Make a bed of crushed ice on a serving platter. Arrange oysters with their liquid in shell halves on ice. Serve with sauces and lemon wedges.

Blini with Caviar

Although tiny black sturgeon roe such as beluga, sevruga, and osetra are classic, gold and orange roe from whitefish and salmon respectively can also be used here. Once fried, the blini can remain in a low (200°F/95°C) oven for up to 30 minutes before topping.

BLINI BATTER

2½ teaspoons (1 package) quick-rise yeast

1¼ cup (10 fl oz/300 ml) milk, heated to 110°F (43°C)

1¼ cups (6½ oz/200 g) all-purpose (plain) flour

2 eggs, separated

About ¼ cup (2 oz/60 g) unsalted butter

1 cup (8 oz/250 g) crème fraîche or sour cream

8 oz (250 g) black caviar, such as beluga, sevruga, or osetra

SERVES 24

1 FOR BLINI BATTER: In a bowl, combine yeast, warm milk, flour, and egg yolks. Stir together to blend and then whisk until smooth. Cover bowl with a kitchen towel and let batter rise in a warm place until doubled in bulk and very spongy in appearance, 2½–3 hours. In a large, perfectly clean bowl, beat egg whites with an electric mixer or whisk until stiff peaks form. Fold into the yeast mixture.

2 In a large nonstick frying pan over low heat, melt about 2 teaspoons of butter. Ladle about 2 tablespoons of batter into the pan for each blini, being careful not to crowd pan. Cook until bottoms are lightly browned and bubbles have formed on the tops, about 3 minutes. Flip blini over and cook until browned on second sides, about 2 minutes longer. Transfer to a warmed platter, cover with aluminum foil, and place in a low oven. Cook remaining blini in the same way, adding butter to pan as needed. You should have about 48 blini in all.

3 To serve, spread about 1 teaspoon crème fraîche over the top of each blini. Top each blini with a scant ½ teaspoon of caviar (see photo, bottom of page 94). Serve at once.

Smoked Salmon, Leek, and Lemon Tartlets

1 recipe Crunch Dough (page 59)

2 tablespoons unsalted butter

2 large leeks, white parts only, trimmed, rinsed, and coarsely chopped

6 tablespoons (3 fl oz/90 ml) crème fraîche

2 tablespoons fresh lemon juice

freshly ground black pepper

¼ lb (125 g) smoked salmon, thinly sliced

½ lemon, thinly sliced and seeded

1½ teaspoons olive oil

MAKES 6 TARTLETS

The time-honored method of baking a pastry shell before it is filled ensures that these tart crusts are nicely golden and cooked through without the filling being curdled.

1 Place 6 tartlet rings, each 4 inches (10 cm) in diameter and about ½ inch (12 mm) deep, on a baking sheet lined with parchment (baking) paper. Divide crunch dough into 6 equal pieces. On a lightly floured work surface, roll out each piece ¼ inch (6 mm) thick and use to line a tartlet ring. Trim edges. Using a fork, prick bases. Cover with plastic wrap and refrigerate for at least 1 hour.

2 In a skillet, melt butter over medium-low heat. Add leeks and cook, stirring often, until tender, about 10 minutes; do not allow to brown. Remove from skillet and let cool.

3 Meanwhile, preheat oven to 425°F (220°C). To blind bake pastry, line chilled pastry shells with aluminum foil, parchment (baking) paper, or waxed paper. Fill with pie weights or uncooked beans or rice. Bake for 10 minutes, then remove lining and weights. Return shells to oven and bake until bottoms are dry and edges are golden, about 5 minutes longer.

4 Mix cooled leeks with crème fraîche and lemon juice. Season to taste with pepper. Spoon leek filling into shells.

5 Bake until filling is set, about 15 minutes. Place smoked salmon in tarts, adding 1 or 2 lemon slices in each. Drizzle with olive oil and return to oven. Bake until salmon is pale pink and firm, about 5 minutes. Serve hot or at room temperature.

Galician-Style Scallops

18 sea scallops, preferably day boat

1 lemon, halved

6 tablespoons (3 fl oz/90 ml) olive oil, plus more for drizzling

1 yellow onion, finely chopped

2 oz (60 g) ham, chopped (about ½ cup)

½ cup (4 fl oz/125 ml) dry white wine

1½ teaspoons *pimentón dulce*

pinch of cayenne pepper

pinch of ground cinnamon

¼ cup (⅓ oz/10 g) chopped fresh flat-leaf (Italian) parsley

salt and freshly ground black pepper

½ cup (2 oz/60 g) fine dried bread crumbs

SERVES 6

You can serve this dish in individual scallop shells or in a single, attractive gratin dish. *Pimentón dulce* is a sweet smoked Spanish paprika that can be found in gourmet markets or spice shops.

1 Preheat oven to 400°F (200°C).

2 Remove tough muscles from scallops, if present. Divide scallops among 6 scallop shells or ramekins and squeeze lemon juice over them.

3 In a skillet, heat 6 tablespoons olive oil over medium heat. Sauté onion and ham until onion is very soft, about 15 minutes. Add wine and cook to reduce slightly, about 5 minutes. Stir in *pimentón dulce*, cayenne, cinnamon, and parsley. Season to taste with salt and black pepper.

4 Top scallops with sauce and bread crumbs. Drizzle with olive oil. Bake until golden and bubbling, about 15 minutes.

Tuna and Green Olive
Empanadas

PASTRY

1¾ cups (9 oz/280 g) all-purpose (plain) flour

1 teaspoon salt

¾ cup (6 oz/185 g) cold unsalted butter, cut into small pieces

4–8 tablespoons (2–4 fl oz/60–125 ml) ice water

FILLING

2 tablespoons olive oil

½ cup (2 oz/60 g) chopped yellow onion

1 can (6 oz/185 g) solid white albacore tuna, drained

¼ cup (1½ oz/45 g) chopped pitted green olives such as Manzanilla

¼ teaspoon *pimentón dulce* (see note, top of page 99)

⅛ teaspoon *each* salt and freshly ground black pepper

1 tablespoon finely chopped fresh flat-leaf (Italian) parsley

1 egg, beaten

SERVES 8

If you don't have time to make the pastry for these empanadas, frozen puff pastry is a quick and easy time-saver that makes this a perfect last-minute hors d'oeuvre. If using puff pastry, be sure to cut the edges very cleanly and keep the egg wash from dribbling over the edges, or the layers will not rise properly.

1 FOR PASTRY: In a bowl, combine flour and salt. Using your fingers or a pastry cutter, cut butter into flour until largest pieces are pea-sized. Using a fork, gradually stir in ice water, 1 tablespoon at a time, until mixture forms a mass. Form dough into a ball and flatten into a disk. Wrap in plastic wrap and refrigerate for 1 hour.

2 FOR FILLING: Meanwhile, heat olive oil in a skillet over medium heat. Add onion and sauté until translucent, about 5 minutes. Add tuna, olives, *pimentón dulce*, salt, pepper, and parsley. Cook, stirring, for 1 minute longer. Remove from heat and transfer to a bowl. Stir in about half of beaten egg.

3 Preheat oven to 375°F (190°C).

4 On a lightly floured work surface, roll out dough into a round 14–15 inches (35–38 cm) in diameter. Using a 3-inch (7.5-cm) round cutter, cut out about 22 dough rounds, rerolling dough scraps as necessary. Roll each round a bit thinner.

5 Spoon 1 heaping teaspoon of tuna filling into center of a dough round. Brush edges with some of beaten egg. Gently fold pastry over filling to make a half-moon. Using tines of a fork, press edges closed and make a few holes in top. Repeat with remaining dough and filling. Place empanadas on a baking sheet and lightly brush with more beaten egg.

6 Bake until crusts are golden brown, 20–25 minutes. Remove from oven and let cool slightly to serve warm, or let cool completely and store in an airtight container for up to 24 hours. Reheat empanadas briefly in oven before serving.

Sizzling Shrimp with Garlic

Known as *gambas al ajillo* in Spain, this tapa is served sizzling, or *pil pileando*, in a little metal pan called a *cazuelita*. Serve with bread for dipping in the garlicky pan juices.

6 tablespoons (3 fl oz/90 ml) olive oil

6 large cloves garlic, finely chopped

1 teaspoon red pepper flakes

1½ teaspoons *pimentón dulce* (see note, top of page 99)

1½ lb (750 g) shrimp (prawns), peeled and deveined, tails left on

⅔ cup (5 fl oz/160 ml) dry white wine

salt and freshly ground black pepper

SERVES 6

1 In a large skillet, heat olive oil over medium heat. Add garlic, red pepper flakes, and *pimentón dulce*. Cook for 1 minute. Stir in shrimp and wine. Raise heat to high and sauté until shrimp are pink, about 3 minutes. Season to taste with salt and black pepper.

Endive Appetizers with Crab

Spoon-shaped endive leaves, both crisp and mildly bitter, are perfect vessels for a range of appetizers, from crème fraîche and caviar to seafood salad. At the market, look for endives that are properly stored away from light—the best will be tightly furled and white, with no brown blemishes or hints of green on the outer leaves.

2 blood oranges

2 heads Belgian endive (chicory/witloof)

1 shallot, finely diced

2 teaspoons Champagne vinegar

3 pinches of salt

3 tablespoons olive oil

½ lb (250 g) fresh lump crabmeat, picked over for shell fragments

3 teaspoons finely snipped fresh chives

freshly ground black pepper

truffle oil

SERVES 4–6

1 Cut a slice off top and bottom of 1 blood orange, then stand it upright. Following contour of fruit, slice off peel and white pith in thick strips. Holding fruit over a bowl, carefully cut along each side of membranes between segments, letting segments and juice drop into bowl. Repeat with remaining orange. Reserve 1 tablespoon juice.

2 Cut off base of each endive, and then separate 16 large leaves. Reserve cones of inner leaves.

3 In a bowl, combine shallot, vinegar, reserved blood orange juice, and salt. Whisk in olive oil.

4 Finely sliver reserved inner cones of endive leaves. In a bowl, toss slivered endive with crabmeat, vinegar mixture, and 2 teaspoons chives. Season to taste with pepper.

5 Mound 1 tablespoon crab mixture on each large outer endive leaf. Add a drop of truffle oil to each mound of crab. Lay 1 blood orange segment next to it. Garnish with remaining chives.

Salmon, Cherry Tomato, and Green Onion Salad

1 lb (500 g) salmon fillet, preferably belly

1½ tablespoons red Hawaiian alaea salt, plus more for serving

1¾ cups (10½ oz/330 g) yellow cherry tomatoes, halved

4 green (spring) onions, including tender green parts, finely chopped

julienned zest of 1 lemon

¼ cup (2 fl oz/60 ml) olive oil

SERVES 2–4

Lomi lomi is a popular Hawaiian preparation in which salmon is soaked in salt water for at least 12 hours, then flaked and combined with tomatoes and green onions. In this version of the dish, the salt has been reduced and the marinating time shortened to 1 hour, for a lighter, fresher salad.

1 Place salmon in a shallow glass dish. Rub 1½ tablespoons alaea salt over salmon. Cover with plastic wrap and refrigerate for 1 hour.

2 Rinse salmon under cold water and pat dry. Remove skin and pin bones. Chop flesh coarsely and transfer to a large bowl.

3 Add tomatoes, green onions, lemon zest, and olive oil to bowl. Mix well. Cover with plastic wrap and refrigerate for 30 minutes.

4 Divide salad among scallop shells or individual bowls. Serve with additional alaea salt alongside for sprinkling.

Salt Cod Purée on Toasts

This specialty of Valencia, Spain, is wonderful served with a sparkling cava wine. Purchase salt cod in Italian markets and well-stocked supermarket fish departments. Delicious served with White-Wine Sangria, page 18.

1 lb (500 g) salt cod

2 small baking potatoes

¾ cup (6 fl oz/180 ml) extra-virgin olive oil

1 tablespoon finely chopped garlic

juice of 1 or 2 lemons

salt and freshly ground black pepper

12 slices coarse country bread, toasted

½ cup (2 oz/60 g) chopped walnuts, toasted

½ cup (¾ oz/20 g) chopped fresh flat-leaf (Italian) parsley

SERVES 6

1 Soak salt cod in cold water in refrigerator for 24–36 hours, changing water at least 4 times. Drain.

2 Place cod in a saucepan and add fresh water to cover. Gradually bring to a gentle simmer over medium-low heat. Reduce heat to low and poach gently until tender, about 10 minutes. Drain and let cool to touch. Break up cod with fingers, discarding any bones, membrane, and tough parts.

3 Meanwhile, preheat oven to 400°F (200°C). Pierce potatoes with a fork. Bake until tender, 45–60 minutes. Let cool, then remove and discard skins. In a bowl, mash potato pulp.

4 In a small saucepan, heat olive oil over low heat. Set aside and keep warm. In a food processor, purée salt cod. Add garlic and process until smooth. With machine running, gradually add warm olive oil and process just until smooth. Transfer to a bowl and stir in mashed potatoes and juice of 1 lemon. If mixture is too stiff, whisk in additional oil or water. Taste and adjust seasoning, if needed, with lemon juice, salt, and pepper.

5 Spread toasted bread with purée and sprinkle with walnuts and parsley. Serve at once.

poultry & meat

So many cuisines have meaty snacks, from dainty bite-sized finger food to more substantial appetizers that require a plate and utensils. Characterized by lively flavors and served with aromatic sauces that make colorful accompaniments, these stylish small dishes delight both the eye and the palate. They complement drinks, stimulate the appetite, stave off hunger, and often end up making a most delicious dinner as the cocktail hour stretches on into the night.

Chicken Liver and Dandelion Salad

BAGUETTE TOASTS

½ thin baguette

¼ cup (2 oz/60 g) unsalted butter, melted

salt and freshly ground black pepper

8 oz (250 g) medium-large dandelion leaves, torn into bite-sized pieces

1 cup (1 oz/30 g) baby dandelion leaves

½ lb (250 g) chicken livers

salt and freshly ground black pepper

1 tablespoon all-purpose (plain) flour

5 tablespoons (2½ fl oz/75 ml) olive oil

¼ lb (125 g) Canadian bacon, cut into thin strips

2 shallots, finely chopped

3 tablespoons red wine vinegar

¼ teaspoon Dijon mustard

pinch of sugar

2 tablespoons sunflower oil

SERVES 4

The unbeatable combination of chicken livers and bacon is the basis for this substantial appetizer. Toasted buttered baguette slices are the required accompaniment. Serve on individual plates with forks.

1 FOR BAGUETTE TOASTS: Preheat oven to 350°F (180°C). Cut baguette on diagonal into 8 slices about ¼ inch (6 mm) thick. Brush both sides of slices with melted butter and season with salt and pepper. Toast on baking sheet in oven for 10 minutes. Set aside.

2 Place mixed dandelion leaves and three quarters of baby dandelion leaves in a large bowl. Reserve remaining baby dandelion leaves.

3 Clean and trim chicken livers, then cut in half. Season livers with salt and pepper, then thinly coat with flour. Set aside.

4 In a sauté pan, heat 2 tablespoons olive oil over medium-high heat. Add Canadian bacon and cook, stirring, until crisp, 5–8 minutes. Transfer bacon to paper towels to drain. Reduce heat to medium-low, add shallots to pan, and cook until soft, 3–5 minutes. Leaving juices in pan, spoon shallots over large dandelion leaves. Add bacon.

5 Raise heat to medium-high and add 1 tablespoon olive oil to juices in sauté pan. Add livers and sauté, turning often, until browned outside but still pink inside, 3–5 minutes. Transfer livers to a plate.

6 Add vinegar to sauté pan and cook over medium-high heat until juices are bubbling, 1–2 minutes. Reduce heat to low and stir in mustard, sugar, sunflower oil, and remaining 2 tablespoons olive oil. Season with salt and pepper. Pour mixture over large dandelion leaves and toss.

7 Divide tossed leaves among 4 individual plates and top each serving with 2 toasted baguette slices. Cut liver halves in half again and spoon over salads. Top with reserved baby dandelion leaves. Serve at once.

Meat-Stuffed Potato Pastries

POTATO DOUGH

2 lb (1 kg) russet potatoes

2 eggs, beaten lightly

1 tablespoon salt

½ teaspoon freshly ground
black pepper

1½ cups (7½ oz/235 g) all-purpose
(plain) flour, plus more for kneading

MEAT FILLING

2 tablespoons olive oil

1 small onion, finely chopped

2 cloves garlic, minced

½ lb (250 g) ground (minced) beef

1 teaspoon salt

½ teaspoon *each* freshly ground
black pepper and ground cinnamon

2 tablespoons chopped fresh
flat-leaf (Italian) parsley

¼ cup (1 oz/30 g) dried white
bread crumbs

1 egg, lightly beaten

1 egg white, lightly beaten

vegetable oil for deep-frying

MAKES ABOUT 20 PASTRIES

With a dough made from potatoes and a filling of ground beef, these hearty fritters from the Sephardic tradition of Jewish cooking are a meal in themselves. If you're running short on time, try microwaving the potatoes instead of baking them. The filling can be made a day ahead of time and stored in the refrigerator in an airtight container, but the pastries should not be fried until you're ready to serve them.

1 FOR DOUGH: Preheat oven to 400°F (200°C). Pierce potatoes with fork, place on oven rack, and bake until very soft, about 1 hour. Let cool to touch.

2 Cut potatoes in half and scoop flesh into a ricer or food mill placed over a bowl. Force flesh through ricer or food mill. Add eggs, salt, pepper, and flour to make a smooth dough. Knead in more flour if it is too wet.

3 FOR FILLING: Heat olive oil in a skillet over medium heat. Add onion and sauté until softened, about 10 minutes. Add garlic and beef. Cook, breaking up meat with a spatula. Stir in salt, pepper, cinnamon, and parsley. Continue to cook until meat is browned, about 10 minutes. Remove from heat. Stir in bread crumbs and egg. Let cool.

4 On a lightly floured surface, roll out dough ⅓ inch (9 mm) thick. Using a 3-inch (7.5-cm) biscuit cutter, cut out rounds. Brush each round with egg white. Place a heaping teaspoon of the meat filling in the center of each circle. Fold each circle in half and press the edges together, sealing securely.

5 In a deep, heavy pot or deep fryer, heat 2 inches (5 cm) oil to 350°F (180°C). Add pastries in batches and fry, turning once, until golden, about 6 minutes total. Using tongs, transfer to paper towels. Serve immediately.

Skewered Vietnamese Beef

The key to this Vietnamese recipe is to get the wok or skillet as hot as possible before adding the beef so that the meat caramelizes quickly. A dipping sauce of black pepper and lime is the perfect complement.

MARINADE

2 tablespoons fresh lime juice

2 tablespoons finely chopped garlic

1 tablespoon fish sauce

2 tablespoons rice vinegar

1 teaspoon sugar

1 lb (500 g) filet mignon, cut into 1-inch (2.5-cm) cubes (about 30)

DIPPING SAUCE

½ cup (4 fl oz/125 ml) fresh lime juice

1 teaspoon kosher salt

1 teaspoon coarsely ground black pepper

1 teaspoon sugar

2 tablespoons canola oil

1 English (hothouse) cucumber, sliced ¼ inch (6 mm) thick and cut into half-moons

SERVES 8

1 FOR MARINADE: In a bowl, combine all marinade ingredients. Pour into a heavy-duty resealable plastic bag.

2 Add beef to bag and seal. Shake to coat well. Let stand at room temperature for 1 hour or refrigerate for up to 4 hours.

3 FOR DIPPING SAUCE: In a small bowl, combine all dipping sauce ingredients. Transfer to a small serving bowl.

4 If beef is refrigerated, remove 30 minutes before cooking. Drain beef. Heat a large nonstick skillet over high heat, add 1 tablespoon oil, and heat until it shimmers. Add half of beef. Let beef cook, undisturbed, until browned, about 1½ minutes. Using tongs, turn beef over and let cook another minute, or until well browned and cooked through. Remove to a plate lined with paper towels. Wipe out pan. Repeat with remaining oil and beef.

5 Thread each piece of beef onto a skewer, followed by a cucumber slice. Place skewers on a platter. Serve at once, accompanied by dipping sauce.

Meatballs with Romesco Sauce

1 lb (500 g) ground (minced) pork

1 cup (2 oz/60 g) fresh bread crumbs

2 eggs, beaten

3 tablespoons chopped fresh flat-leaf
(Italian) parsley

3 cloves garlic, finely chopped

¼ cup (1¼ oz/37 g) pine nuts

½ teaspoon *each* salt and freshly
ground black pepper

⅛ teaspoon ground cinnamon

1–2 tablespoons olive oil

ROMESCO SAUCE

½ cup (3 oz/90 g) whole almonds

½ lb (250 g) tomatoes

1 tablespoon olive oil

1 large slice white bread

¼ teaspoon red pepper flakes

1 clove garlic, chopped

½ cup (3 oz/90 g) pimientos, drained

¼ teaspoon *each* paprika, salt, and
freshly ground black pepper

¼ cup (2 fl oz/60 ml)
red wine vinegar

½ cup (4 fl oz/125 ml) olive oil

SERVES 6

Don't let the word "meatballs" fool you. With a touch of cinnamon and pine nuts added to the ground pork, these tasty morsels are superb. Typically, a Spanish romesco sauce is made only with Spanish pimientos, a type of sweet red pepper, but this recipe also calls for tomatoes, which give the sauce a nice tang.

1 In a bowl, combine pork, bread crumbs, eggs, parsley, garlic, pine nuts, salt, pepper, and cinnamon. Form into 1-inch (2.5-cm) balls.

2 In a skillet, heat oil over medium heat. Working in batches to avoid crowding, sauté meatballs until well browned, about 5 minutes. Transfer to paper towels to drain.

3 FOR ROMESCO SAUCE: Spread almonds on a baking sheet and toast in a 350°F (180°C) oven until lightly browned and fragrant. Transfer to a plate.

4 Bring a saucepan of water to a boil. Using a sharp knife, score a shallow X in blossom end of each tomato. Immerse tomatoes in the boiling water and leave for 15–30 seconds, or until skins just begin to wrinkle. Remove tomatoes with a slotted spoon, let cool slightly, then peel away skins. Cut in half crosswise and squeeze gently to dislodge seeds.

5 Heat olive oil in a skillet over medium heat. Fry bread until golden on both sides, about 1 minute. In a food processor, finely chop bread, almonds, red pepper flakes, and garlic. Add pimientos, tomatoes, paprika, salt, and pepper. Process to a smooth paste. Add vinegar and process to combine. With machine running, gradually add olive oil in a thin stream to make an emulsified sauce.

6 Transfer meatballs to a serving plate. Serve with romesco sauce.

Stuffed Figs on Salami

This unusual combination teams the saltiness of salami and the tang of goat cheese with the sweetness of pistachios and figs. Choose figs that are soft to the touch, which have the fully developed sugars lacking in firm figs.

¼ cup (1 oz/30 g) pistachios, coarsely chopped

12 ripe figs

1½ tablespoons extra-virgin olive oil

¼ cup (1 oz/30 g) soft goat cheese

12 thin slices soppressata or other dried Italian salami

SERVES 6

1 Preheat oven to 400°F (200°C).

2 In a frying pan, toast pistachios over medium heat, shaking pan, until fragrant, about 3 minutes. Be careful not to burn them. Set aside.

3 Rub figs all over with olive oil, then make a lengthwise slit in each fig and insert 1 teaspoon cheese in each. Place figs, slit end up, on a baking sheet.

4 Bake until figs are plump and shiny but have not burst, about 10 minutes.

5 Meanwhile, place two slices of soppressata on each small plate. To serve, place a fig on top of each slice of soppressata.

index

acknowledgments

Special thanks to the many talented authors and photographers who contributed so greatly to this book. Also, thanks to Peggy Fallon, Tanya Henry, Joan Olson, Victoria Spencer, Richard Van Oosterhout, and Renée Myers for their valuable assistance.

credits

AUTHORS: **Brigit Binns:** Page 96; **Giuseppe Cipriani:** Page 27; **Sara Deseran:** Pages 78, 100, 121; **Joyce Goldstein:** Pages 18 (all), 75, 85, 89, 99, 105, 110, 116; **Andy Harris:** Pages 17, 21 (all), 31, 35, 36 (all), 39 (all), 48, 53 (all), 54, 82, 90, 109; **Jeffry Lindenmuth:** Pages 22, 28; **Deborah Madison:** Pages 63, 67, 71, 106; **Donata Maggiapinto:** Pages 40, 93; **Pascal Rigo:** Pages 59, 64, 97; **Staff:** Pages 43 (bottom), 44, 125; **Susie Theodorou:** Pages 60, 72, 81, 115; **Marimar Torres:** Page 122; **Jean-Georges Vongerichten:** Page 43 (top).

PHOTOGRAPHERS: **Quentin Bacon:** Pages 34, 68 (top left, top right), 79, 101, 120; **Leigh Beisch:** Pages 84, 117; **Maren Caruso:** Page 102; **Beatriz da Costa:** Pages 62, 70; **Ben Dearnley:** Page 103; **Miki Duisterhof:** Pages 73, 80; **Dana Gallagher:** Pages 58, 65; **Lisa Hubbard:** Page 114; **Richard Jung:** Page 77; **David Loftus:** Pages 8, 9, 24, 25, 26, 32 (top left), 33, 124; **William Meppem:** Pages 1, 6, 12, 16, 19, 20 (all), 29, 30, 32 (top right, bottom left, bottom right), 37 (all), 38, 42, 49, 52 (all), 55, 61, 68 (bottom left, bottom right), 69, 74, 83, 88, 91, 95, 98, 104, 107, 108, 111, 118, 119, 123; **Minh+Wass:** endpapers; **Amy Neunsinger:** Pages 41, 45, 92; **David Prince:** Pages 66; **Roger Stowell:** Pages 10, 50 (all), 51; **Luca Trovato:** Page 23; **Lisa Charles Watson:** Page 94 (all); **Simon Wheeler:** Page 76 (all); **Anna Williams:** Page 13.

WILLIAMS-SONOMA INC.
Founder & Vice Chairman: Chuck Williams

WILLIAMS-SONOMA TASTE
Editor-in-Chief: Andy Harris
Art Director: Emma Ross
Original Design: Martin Welch

WELDON OWEN INC.
Chief Executive Officer: John Owen
President and Chief Operating Officer: Terry Newell
Vice President International Sales: Stuart Laurence
Sales Manager: Emily Jahn
Creative Director: Gaye Allen
Publisher: Hannah Rahill
Associate Publisher: Val Cipollone
Art Director: Kari Ontko, India Ink
Assistant Editor: Juli Vendzules
Copy Editor: Desne Ahlers
Proofreader: Carrie Bradley
Indexer: Ken DellaPenta
Production: Chris Hemesath, Teri Bell

Recipes and photographs originally published in the USA, 2000-2002, in Williams-Sonoma TASTE Magazine © 2000–2002 Weldon Owen Magazines Inc. and Williams-Sonoma Inc.

COCKTAILS & APPETIZERS
Conceived and produced by Weldon Owen Inc.
814 Montgomery Street, San Francisco, CA 94133
In collaboration with Williams-Sonoma Inc.
3250 Van Ness Avenue, San Francisco, CA 94109

Printed in China by Midas Printing Limited

A WELDON OWEN PRODUCTION

First printed in 2005
10 9 8 7 6 5 4 3 2 1

Library of Congress Cataloging-in-Publication Data is available
ISBN 1-740895-27-4